Launcher of Lists

Disclaimer

This e-book has been written for information purposes only. Every effort has been made to make this ebook as complete and accurate as possible. However, there may be mistakes in typography or content. Also, this e-book provides information only up to the publishing date. Therefore, this ebook should be used as a guide - not as the ultimate source.

The purpose of this ebook is to educate. The author and the publisher does not warrant that the information contained in this e-book is fully complete and shall not be responsible for any errors or omissions. The author and publisher shall have neither liability nor responsibility to any person or entity with respect to any loss or damage caused or alleged to be caused directly or indirectly by this e-book.

Launcher of Lists

Table of Contents

Introduction

Everyone, or at least every one among us, knows just how important it is to build a list of e-mail addresses for a good Internet marketing. Now, many budding Internet marketers today make the wasteful mistake of overlooking their single most powerful tool – the list of e-mail addresses they have compiled.

Think about it. You already have the e-mail addresses of the people who may be interested in what you have to offer. So why not sell them related stuff via those e-mail addresses? They gave you the consent to use them for communication, after all. Of course, you should know your limitations too, but that's another discussion altogether.

Of course, you don't just come up with a list of e-mail addresses. It takes time and the consent of the people. That is where this book comes in. You are holding, in a manner of speaking, the guidebook to a better Internet marketing business. This will help you build your list via various techniques, detailed across 77 tips.

Well then, now we can get started. A lot of these techniques are what you might think of as different tools in the Internet marketing toolbox, but remember that the tool is much more effective if used in a certain manner. Without further ado, let's kick off with tip number 1.

Tips

Tip Number 1: Blogging is king.

More precisely, regular blog posting is king.

Starting a blog of your own can be easy or difficult, depending on how you go about it. The hard way would be to start one from scratch using good old web page coding – which is more trouble than it is worth really. The easy way is to use some sort of automation in the set-up. WordPress is one such tool of choice. It works on plug-ins and templates, so you can create a customized look without the problems that go with all the coding that you would need otherwise.

If you can post a blog entry once a day, then you are doing well enough. That means that you will be generating leads and adding to your list every day.

Tip Number 2: Stay relevant.

Whether you are posting blog entries or sending e-mails to the addresses on your list, you need to stay on topic – that is, maintain focus on the very thing that got people interested in you in the first place.

When you stray too far from the topic of interest, people will start skipping over what you send them. Later on, they will start marking your messages as spam, and you can kiss their patronage goodbye. It's okay to make a few side mentions, but overall you need to stay on track.

If you do mention something on the side, make sure that it is easily skippable without destroying the essence of the whole. Using proper paragraphing can achieve this effect. Additionally, inserting these extra bits in footer sections can work too.

Tip Number 3: Make a proper squeeze page.

A squeeze page is a simple straightforward web page built with the intention of getting the visitors to give you their e-mail addresses (an action known as "opt-in").

Remember that the squeeze page is not a page for selling your products. What a squeeze page does is "squeezing" the e-mail addresses, and not money, out of visitors. Therefore, you can save the actual links to sales and purchases for later. All you need to put into a squeeze page is the premise of your service, and a little bit of pre-selling. Think of it as posting the headlines and first few lines of the newspaper.

Tip Number 4: Skip the video on squeeze pages, or people will skip over you.

Why is this so, you ask? Isn't video a good way of generating leads and convincing visitors? Well, yes, but think about where you put it!

The fact is that most people who visit your squeeze page and opt-in are the impulsive type. That also means that they are not exactly patient. Even with high-speed broadband that is available nowadays, people still do not like waiting for anything to load if they are not sure they want it.

By keeping your squeeze pages free of videos, you will allow it to load quickly and cleanly. Your visitors can get to read the salient points right away, and they will opt in while their attentions are aflame.

Tip Number 5: No heavyweight effects on your squeeze page

In addition to keeping videos away from your squeeze page, you should also avoid media that consume high bandwidths. Sounds and music are definitely out, since they will hold up the loading process. Make sure to trim and compress images that you use on your page. Don't bother with flashy Flash effects.

In any case, smarter users do block media from untrusted sources, so your special effects are simply left out. As such, you should just stick to text and graphics, so you do not lose any impact.

Tip Number 6: Use video in your posts!

YouTube has made publishing videos of yourself a breeze, and it is free. This means you can get a stronger connection with your audience without paying an additional cent!

Adding videos to blog posts makes them more capable of making an impact, especially if you have some good looks. Some people prefer to read, others like to watch and listen. By including a video in your well-written blog posts, you can generate leads from several types of people. Make sure to make yourself presentable before going on-cam.

Tip Number 7: Video responses are cool

Another application of videos in marketing blogs is as a means of responding to the most important questions. It makes your followers think that you really do care about what they think and ask – and you do, considering the effort you took to post videos for them.

Picking out the questions that matter most is the tricky part. It is unlikely that you will be able to answer all the questions when your following grows beyond a certain point. Additionally, you should discuss only questions related to the main topic, and relegate questions regarding problems about site features (like glitches) to text responses.

Another way that this could work in your favor is that your responses generate traffic and boost your popularity. Then, people who aren't following you will check out the videos, and if they like what they see, they'll check out your other videos, and it snowballs from there.

Tip Number 8: RSS is your BFF

RSS is usually expanded as "Really Simple Syndication" and it really is simple. The idea of using RSS is that it can publish your media to any RSS reader "tuned in" to your feed. That means that when you post something, whether it is a text blog entry, a video, or an audio podcast, then those who chose to receive RSS data from you will get an update on their RSS readers. It's like they get a personal notification every time you put something up online.

Tip Number 9: You can substitute audio for video

Speaking of podcasts, audio is a viable substitute. If you are not quite confident about your looks, or want to keep your online footprint as small as you can, then going with audio instead of video may be the solution. It helps to have a good voice, but the most important advantage of audio over video is that it consumes less space and can therefore be downloaded more quickly. There are some things that you can't do with audio, but it does have many of the communication capabilities of video.

Tip Number 10: SEO is FTW

SEO stands for "Search Engine Optimization", a set of ideas and procedures meant to shape search engine traffic to your benefit as an Internet marketer. In theory, you will fix your webpages in such a way that search engines (like Google and Yahoo!) will favor your site and feature it higher among results for relevant searches.

In practice though, SEO is pretty complex, and will have to be discussed elsewhere. It is also constantly changing, so keeping up is pretty tough, but the payoff is well worth the trouble.

Tip Number 11: Stay human, get human attention

In as much as you are running or starting up an Internet marketing business, you need to remember that people are not leads; they are people. If you do not approach them with the intention of helping them, they will not be likely to bother noticing you. Remember that you are dealing with human beings. Be fair, be helpful, and be human. It will be that much better for you and for everyone in the end.

Helping does not mean that it has to be free, but the fact remains that you are offering something that can make life easier for your audience.

Tip Number 12: Freebies, freebies!

Everybody loves free stuff, as long as you're not pushy about it – then it becomes suspicious. Whatever type of business you have, it pays to give some stuff or services away. Whether it is a regular freebie or a periodic blowout, there must be something you can give away to people.

Many marketers give away free stuff when people sign up. At times, there are also free items or samples with no obligation to register. Tempting visitors by giving them a taste is as old a marketing strategy as marketing itself. If the visitors are suitably impressed, then you can be quite sure that they will opt into your list.

Tip Number 13: Tag team!

One way to get a leg up in Internet marketing is to give a hand to other marketers. It makes sense, as long as you both keep your respective ends of the bargain. There are many ways to apply this cooperative principle, and we will discuss them across several tips. The first would be to feature links to each other's webpages under a "related info" or similar section on your homepage. If you do not deal in the same type of product or service, then the section can be labeled something like "Friends", "Partners", or "Other Cool Stuff".

Tip Number 14: Tag team tactic: follow-up!

This is an interesting tactic when it comes to making sales. For example, you finish a transaction with a customer. At the receipt page, you insert an offer for a friendly competitors' product or service. If you do make a sale, you can get a commission from your competitor, and he can do the same for you. It generates leads both ways! The best part is that you do not even have to be offering the same type of goods or services!

Tip Number 15: Tag team tactic: big blowout!

Small giveaways do create buzz, but not as much as big blowouts, right? Well, you can team up with other Internet marketers to organize some sort of event with free giveaways, whether online or in meatspace (the "real" world). It creates buzz for all of your marketing businesses, plus it has a

bigger profile and presence. This produces leads in many ways, and also
helps you make friends and partners.

Tip Number 16: Tag team tactic: sponsor!

Sponsoring local bands, sports teams, or other such public entities is a
great way of boosting your presence, but it can be a bit tough to come up
with some reasonable amount. Teaming up with other interested Internet
marketers can make it easier for all of you to get the word out without
paying through the nose.

**Tip Number 17: Facebook, MySpace, and other page-based social
networks work**

These social networking services are great because you can do a lot of
different things on them. Still, if the point is to build up your list, you have to
remember to make it interesting, especially towards the target audience.
Don't just add people willy-nilly. Pick out the ones with interests related to
what you have to offer, and build a network on the people who are
interested. It is much more efficient and synergistic in some ways.

Tip Number 18: Microblogging services like Twitter, Plurk, et cetera

The micro format is actually pretty useful. In fact, if you sue it right, you can
use this to get some real-time leverage for your business.

You can use the framework to drive people to your squeeze page, or use it to make announcements of new blog posts. Of course, at its core you can use it to meet new people who are interested in the goods or services that you can offer.

Tip Number 19: Article marketing articulates your page and the casual readers

Writing articles and submitting them to various sites across the Web can make a big positive impact on your business. In fact, you can use these articles to entice people who may have had only a passing interest in what you have to offer.

Of course, it is important to have decent writing skills. It is not just about spelling and grammar. You also have to have a way with words that either overrides reason or steers it towards your direction. In other words, your charisma in writing is an essential element for this tactic.

Tip Number 20: Forums can enclose, stimulate, and multiply your followers

Internet forums are great because people can converse (not in real-time) by means of posted messages.

That means other people can read what's been going on and make their own comments.

You can join forums and dive into related threads or start new topics. Better yet, you can start up your own forum! It doesn't take much – just a Web host and an automated forum website builder.

Forums are not just for discussing matters with members. They also make great places to meet people, and more importantly, meet people who are already interested in the raison d'etre of the forum.

Tip Number 21: Joint ventures in lead generation?

You bet! Joining forces may be quite common in Internet marketing activities, but it is not so in lead generation. This is a shame, since it can work very well for lead generation!

For example, you have a list of people that you e-mail regularly and they have not bought anything from you. Why not try selling them another marketer's products or services? You can generate leads for your ally and they can do the same for you. It can generate traffic both ways, which makes it all good in the end.

Tip Number 22: Ning.com is a major social networking system

Though it may not have as large a following as the near-legendary Facebook, Ning is great because it provides the framework to start up social networking pages on any topic of interest.

The idea is to set up the network and the premise, and watch as people join and get each other fired up by talking about the topic of interest. You're likely to get a group of like-minded people with this tactic.

Tip Number 23: Traffic Geyser builds up your steam

Traffic Geyser is a piece of software that links in with the video component of your enterprise. After recording a video, you need to upload it into a video hosting service like YouTube, otherwise it just sits on your hard drive doing nothing. Uploading to one or two such sites is easy enough. What about if you have a half-dozen or more video sites to upload to?

That's where Traffic Geyser comes in. It can upload your video to various video hosting websites across the Web automatically. That means spending less time waiting for uploads to finish so you can upload the next one. Moreover, it also works with non-video content, such as articles, blog posts, and more.

Tip Number 24: Pay-per-click advertising means better opt-in conversion

PPC or pay-per-click advertising gets your ad out across the Web, which are displayed on appropriate Web pages. An interesting PPC ad can get people to click it and get redirected to your squeeze page, opt-in page, or any other page that you link it to.

The best part is that people will only click on your ad if they see something that interests them. By reaching your chosen page via these ads, they basically qualify themselves as persons interested in the item on offer.

Tip Number 25: BuddyPress!

You might not heard of this little WordPress plug-in before, but it is incredibly powerful. It actually helps you set up a social network on your own Webpage running on WordPress! Just add the plug-in to your local instance of WordPress, and with a few clicks and tweaks you have yourself a functioal social networking system!

Tip Number 26: SocialGO

It is another social networking system, and is a direct competitor of Ning. This is also a good choice for setting up social networks under your thumb, so check it out and think about how you can use it to your own benefit.

Tip Number 27: Press releases aren't just for big companies or for celebrities

In fact, you, the Internet marketer, can make great use of it. Whenever you are putting out a new product or service, or announcing some modification to pricing or limited-time offers, a press release can get you heard and noticed.

There are several ways to achieve this, and they generate a whole lot of back links to your page. One way it to convert an article into a press release, stick in your squeeze page URL, and publish.

Tip Number 28: Tell a Friend!

Tell a friend – or get your visitors to tell their friends! You can get your visitors to tell their friends and share what you have to offer by adding a tell-a-friend form in various strategic locations on your pages. Say right after confirming opt-in or purchases, or always close at hand on the sidebar.

Of course, if you insert it so that it appears automatically, make sure that your visitors are allowed to skip it. No one likes being forced to do anything, after all.

Tip Number 29: Sell on eBay.

Even if what you are offering is really cheap or even free, eBay makes a great launching point for sales and giveaways. It has all the essential framework components in place, so all you have to do is register and put your item up "for sale". Whether it is a digital product or a material object, you can sell it here.

Tip Number 30: Amazon.com works just like eBay, but with a focus towards books – digital or material

It can be a digital book, a white paper, or even an audio book. In addition to that, you can produce material in Kindle-compatible formats. Since the Kindle is getting good buzz and represents a rising trend, you can make a killing with this method.

Tip Number 31: "Customer squeeze"

In essence this is a combination of selling a product and getting the customer to opt-in, all in one go. The act of purchasing becomes the act of opting in too! Just make sure that you explicitly state what the process involves, since not everyone will be pleased by the automatic opt-in.

Tip Number 32: E-zine advertising is easy advertising

E-zines are regular digital magazine publications, and they make for good places to put your ads. Of course, the target audience of the magazine should dovetail reasonably with your target demographic, otherwise it is just a waste of time and money.

One good thing about this is that if you can find an e-zine that works well with your offered goods or services, people who subscribe to the e-zine will have qualified themselves as people who are interested in what you have.

Tip Number 33: Digital classified ads

Similar in concept to e-zine advertising, the idea is to post your ad and have someone publish it for you. The primary downside is that your ad can "get lost" amongst the many types of ads, some of which will be competing directly with yours. Still, digital classified ads are reasonably cheap and pretty easy. Just search for "digital classified ads" and your favorite search engine will pull up at least a couple of services for you.

Tip Number 34: Printed classified ads.

A good old standby, printed ads in newspapers and the like may seem old-fashioned, but it does work well enough. It all depends on your target audience.

Tip Number 35: Banner ads

Banner ads are great because they can get your ads on a variety of websites and webpages which bear some relation to your field of interest. Different advertisers feature different prices and scopes, so it pays to do some of your own research and fine-tune your choice for banner advertising.

Tip Number 36: Advertising on foot!

If you think posting ads in the newspaper is old-fashioned, then this one is even more old-fashioned. In fact, it's so old-fashioned, it's now novel again, just like how "retro" seems to become fashionable every few decades.

The idea here is to post print ads in various locations, such as public bulletin boards and the like. Some coffee shops and similar establishments have something like a public bulletin board, so they could be good places to start. Remember to post your ads only where you are allowed! There's little point in posting if they'll only get torn down in short order.

Of course, you should talk to people too. If you notice someone reading your ads, walk up to them with a simple smile, introduce yourself and ask whether or not the ad interests them. Remember to approach them with confidence and intent, but not to the point of being pushy.

Tip Number 37: Business cards

Since you will be talking with people personally, business cards are in order. It makes introducing yourself easier, and can transmit contact information without effort. It also makes you look more professional and may impress ordinary people. Additionally, it can remind people of you every time they see it.

Good business card design is a different matter, of course, and will not be discussed here.

Tip Number 38: Word of mouth advertising

The oldest form of advertising there is, it is almost as old as language itself. The best strength that this style of advertising has is the strength of recommendation as a result of personal relationships. Think about it:

would you believe a friend or a stranger when it comes to recommendations for a good restaurant? How about when it comes to what garage does good body work? People are inherently social, and will put more weight on the judgment of people they know than otherwise. Of course, the best way to stir up a buzz with word-of-mouth advertising is to provide good service or products. It will come naturally and truthfully, which works out for the best for all of us.

Tip Number 39: Exit pop-ups are pop-ups that appear as visitors leave a website or Web page

In this context, the idea is to generate leads for some other venture. You can insert these exit pop-ups on your own page's or someone else's pages, as long as you have their permission. You can then direct the exiting visitor to your target website.

Tip Number 40: Radio ads can work for business ventures with a local scope

It does not take a whole lot to advertise on local radio, so drop by your local radio station and ask them about it.

Tip Number 41: Online radio advertising is a step up from the old radio advertising

Online radio has a wider reach, which makes it more useful for enterprises whose scopes cover more than just their immediate locale. The online radio format itself is not super-popular yet, but it is indeed a rising trend.

Tip Number 42: Book inserts

Amazon and some other vendors offer this service. Book inserts are small ads (leaflets and the like) included with books that are shipped out to buyers. This is great especially if the book that was ordered bears some connection to your topic of interest. You can get the impulsive buyer's notice this way.

Tip Number 43: Cost Per Action advertising

In Cost Per Action advertising, you (as a marketer) pay the advertising entity a given amount for a set action performed by customers. This action usually involves a purchase of some sort. The action in question is not limited to just purchasing though, as CPA advertising can also cover actions like filling out forms and the like.

Some like CPA advertising because they only pay for those actions that actually produce a profit for them, viz, you pay them something like a commission. In fact, it might be easier to think of it as a commission-based transaction.

Tip Number 44: Cost Per Lead advertising

Cost Per Lead advertising is a form of advertising where the marketer
(that's you) pays a given amount any time you get viable customer
information from the intermediary entity (service provider).

CPL is a different in that it is better used when trying to contact customers
on multiple fronts, like newsletters, direct mail, et cetera. This might
actually be better for building up your list than CPA, which works better for
selling your products.

Tip Number 45: Autoresponders with a difference!

Autoresponders are computer programs or services that send e-mails
automatically based on your autresponder schedule. By modifying the
response mechanisms, you can insert links to other webpages, whether
they are your own, or someone else's.

You can create cross traffic between websites that you own, or exchange
links with allied marketers (which works even better). It's one way that the
Golden Rule is applied in the context of Internet marketing.

Tip Number 46: Vimeo is a good alternative to YouTube

It also has a less "spammy" quality than YouTube, though it is by no means
immune to the inane and stupid things that some people post online.

Tip Number 47: Viddler

Viddler is another alternative video hosting website, with the same strengths and shortcomings of YouTube.

Tip Number 48: Direct mail, direct connection.

Direct mail is one way to get your business noticed by target communities. You can write letters and put them in envelopes, or go with simple postcard-type mail.

You will undoubtedly lose some when people filter out the junk mail, but you can be sure that at least some of them will see and at least read through your letter. That's why direct mail needs to be done in bulk.

Tip Number 49: Bulky mail.

This one may seem like a prank, but it does get the job done! The idea is to send direct mail, but with something large and bulky inside the envelope – thus the name "bulky mail". It's like finding ping pong balls in an envelope. These letters will surely get opened!
The question lies in whether people will think that you have a sense of humor or if you are just messing around with them. You'll have to make the accompanying letter pretty convincing!

Tip Number 50: SMS advertising.

It might seem like a bit of a bother to send out SMS to truckloads of people, but you get an advantage that e-mail and other type of mail don't – when people receive a text message, they are notified in real time. Whereas other type of messages are only checked when available time rolls around, a text message is often read immediately since the receivers' cellphones notify them as it arrives.

Some cellphones are capable of running programs that send SMSs automatically. This means that you can set up a template, then provide a list of names and the like. Such programs are not easy to find though. On the other hand, there are PC-based programs that send SMSs, which may be an easier option.

Tip Number 51: Traffic exchanges can help you get traffic.

After joining a traffic exchange, you will then need to browse through other members' webpages and in doing so you will earn credits. These credits can then be used to get traffic for your own submitted website, and the cycle continues.

Tip Number 52: List builder sites help you get e-mail addresses for your own list.

Of course, this could just as easily be made into a lead generation method, wherein you will send e-mails to those e-mail addresses that you got. One example list builder sites is www.ViralURL.com

Tip Number 53: Ads IRL.

IRL stand for "In Real Life", so in this case we are talking about ads with a physical presence. The basic idea is to print a stack of flyers and posters, then slap them wherever a chance presents itself.

Some good places to stick these are in hallways and in toilet stalls. Hallways always have people moving through them, so simpler ads with less text are recommended. In toilet stalls, you can be a bit more verbose since people will be taking a bit of time to do their thing. Your ad will become worthy reading material, and might prove useful if the toilet paper runs out. Just kidding – or not.

Tip Number 54: Social bookmarking.

Sites like Digg, Reddit, and StumbleUpon are what are called social bookmarking sites. These sites basically allow users to mark certain pages on the Web and share these bookmarks with fellow registered users and casual visitors. Then, as more people mark the page positively or negatively, its position of prominence on the social bookmarking site will change.

It is in a way a social thermometer for the popularity and interesting qualities of a Web page. You can get you page in the lists, and if it's set up well, then you might see a meteoric rise in popularity!

Tip Number 55: Viral PDF works in a way similar to viral videos, though it is not quite as big a deal

The concept lies in writing a PDF file with useful information and spreading it amongst networks and individual people. If it proves interesting or useful enough, they'll then share it with their friends and acquaintances, and those people will do the same, and so on and so forth.

Why a PDF? PDF stands for Portable Document Format. It can be read on a wide variety of devices and platforms, plus can be secured for both the protection of intellectual property and against malicious attachments. It serves as a secure format for both the giver and the receiver.

Tip Number 56: Yahoo! Answers.

Yahoo! Answers is a site where people can ask questions and get answers from the members of the community. The idea is that people will post relevant items that answer the questions. In your case, you should search for questions that you can answer, post a reply, and then stick your business URL in the footer. If you can find questions that relate directly to your field of business interest, then all the better, because you can stick your URL inline as part of the answer.

Tip Number 57: Micropatronage?

This is basically a term that was invented to refer to the online equivalent of an ages-old activity – asking for money for your performances. Basically, you ask visitors and watchers to donate money to you, since you gave some sort of performance for free.

A good example is the model used by webcomic authors. The webcomics are free for anyone to view, but you have the option of donating to the author (via PayPal, et cetera) to "keep the webcomic going". It's like dropping a coin into a street performer's hat. Now, this works to build your list because you get identity information from donations!

Tip Number 58: Crowd funding aka crowd financing aka crowd-sourced capital

Related to micropatronage, but different, crowd funding is the concept of getting grassroots-level people to send and pool resources to be used to some end. The goal may be things like disaster relief, or support for a new invention, or political campaign funds, or in your case of interest, support for a startup company.

There are several models to how this is executed, which may involve some money-back guarantee to the people who gave their money. For example, if the target amount is not reached, the funds held in escrow will be returned. If you really want to make this work, then you will need to feed the buzz to fill the tank, so to speak.

Tip Number 59: Google Knol – what's a knol?

Well, Google is passing the "knol" off as "the unit of knowledge". Questions of branding and naming aside, Google Knol is Google's answer to the concept of a collection of user-submitted articles, categorized and indexed by topic.

Google seems to be getting its hands into every cookie jar in the house that is the Internet - don't bother thinking about how many hands it has. Some people argue that it is like Wikipedia, others argue against that argument. Google is trying to prevent the vandalism that Wikipedia faces by requiring real identities for user accounts (which may be verified by phone or credit card number). In theory, this should make the organic database to be more truthful and unbiased.

For you though, it can be just another way of publishing articles and getting yourself noticed. Check it out when you have the time.

Tip Number 60: Commenting on blogs and other online content

This is a good way to get the word out about your business, but be warned – if your reply is irrelevant to the subject of the posted content then you face the problem of being marked as a spammer. Keep your comments intelligent and relevant, then insert your URL as a footer or in the comment content if it is strongly relevant.

No one likes spam, so don't make the same mistake as so many other aspiring Internet marketers.

Tip Number 61: ShareThis and AddThis

These are blog plug-ins that allow people to share links to your Web pages on social networks with just a few clicks. In principle, it is like allowing users to recommend your webpage to their friends, with the convenience of one or a couple of clicks.

Of course, sharing links could be done by copying the URL in the address bar and pasting it into your social network posts, but that's inelegant and sometimes doesn't quite work out. With these plug-ins or widgets, you will make it easier for visitors to share and recommend your pages. Remember – the easier you make it for people, the more likely they are to do it.

Tip Number 62: Write a newsletter!

Whether in meatspace or in cyberspace, your newsletter can get casual readers interested and keep current subscribers in the loop. Include useful tips and information in addition to informing the reader of what's new and what's trending. A bit of humor is usually appreciated.

Tip Number 63: Guest writing!

Now this is a cool and fun activity that works very well to improve your own popularity. You can write an article or blog post and post it on someone else's blog! You'll be riding on the coattails of their popularity, while they in turn can gain popularity from your work. Plus, lots of people like crossovers.

The only visible bump on the road is of course getting the blog owner to allow you to post an article. You will need to make friends with the blog owner, which is not unrewarding in itself.

Tip Number 64: Mini-jobs via Amazon Mechanical Turk.

Yeah, it sounds crazy until you know the source of the name (just Google "the Turk" or "the Mechanical Turk"). The premise of the service is that you post simple job requests that pay equivalently small amounts of money. Then, people looking to make an extra buck will log-in, browse through the job requests, perform them, and get paid.

The requested tasks vary. Some might ask people to pick the best picture out of a group. Others might pay for people to answer surveys. In your case, you can pay people to opt into your list!

Tip Number 65: Submit your site to directories.

We are referring specifically to Web directories like Yahoo! Directories, not your local yellow pages. Those of a more organized and step-by-step mindset will likely turn to these services when they are in need of something. If that something happens to be related to your field of interest, then their searches will likely pull up your website! Old concept, new technology, as with so many other things.

Tip Number 66: Give interviews.

Yet another way of getting your presence known to the public and improving your apparent wisdom, giving interviews is for the bold and confident. People who share interests in your particular niche can benefit from listening to what a more experienced practitioner can share – and that could be you!

You will need to cultivate an image that won't rub them the wrong way, and is also in keeping with your other material. After all, it would be strange to watch or listen to someone who seems boisterous and peppy, but whose written works are somber and flat, or vice versa.

Tip Number 67: Written tutorials and instructional articles.

Writing tutorials and submitting them to article aggregation websites can be easy and effective, if you know what you are talking about. Getting specific instructions on what to do can help make many things easier, and so people are on a constant lookout for these.

Now, if you can write tutorials and other instructional materials and publish them for public access, you are essentially showing people how knowledgeable you are – and thus improving your trustworthiness. Your user profile on these aggregation websites can include URLs to your webpages, and again you can include the URLs in your articles if it is relevant.

Tip Number 68: Video demonstrations and tutorials.

By extension, instructional and demonstrative videos can achieve the same if not a better effect. It has the useful information that people value, and gives them a better look into who you are.   It's all about showing people that you know what you are talking about and that you want to help them in whatever way you can. They'll eat it up!

Tip Number 69: Google Buzz is a simplified social networking framework owned by Google

The idea is to get people to talk about stuff that interests them. Connect with people who share interests, and get in the conversation. Be interesting, not obnoxious. At opportune times, share your links, and get those opt-ins.

Tip Number 70: Google AdSense is an advertising service from Google

It works because it delivers the right ads based on the type of webpage being viewed. That means that your ads only appear on pages that are related to your topic, so you get a better click-through and conversion rate. Tip Number 71: Buy someone else's website

Yeah, it sounds like a corporate takeover, and it might as well be. This works because you can then change your newly-acquired website to suit your needs. Whether you build it up as a separate product or use it to link back to your own website is up to you.

The idea is that you are trying to get the traffic that the purchased site was getting. At the very least, you can include the list of contacts in the declaration of sale, so you can build your list directly.

Tip Number 72: Buy expired domain traffic

Similar to buying someone else's website, but also distinct. Expired domains are basically webpage addresses that were used but now are no longer in use. Think of what happens to a brand when the company drops it or falls altogether. People will remember the brand, and might look for it even after the company is gone.

In the context of the Web, when a site goes permanently offline, the domain no longer directs users to the website. As such, they are lost, and that traffic is wasted. Now if you could redirect that traffic to your website, then that works for you!

Tip Number 73: Join a webring

In the earlier days of the Internet, webrings were more popular. Today, they are less popular but not by any means extinct. The idea is that you will join or form a group of websites with a common navigation menu. When users click buttons on this menu, they are taken from one site to the next, or previous, such that they move in a circuit around the ting of websites. As a failsafe, there is usually a central node that can redirect visitors should a member of the webring go offline.

Joining a webring can work to your favor. Say a visitor is looking for something. While your webring allies may offer the same thing as you do, the visitor may not like the presentation that they have, and will eventually land on your page – you see where this is going.

Tip Number 74: Do your own street-level advertising.

Add a sticker to your car that points to your website. Yeah, it might not work very well, but remember that if you never try, you'll never win! You will want to make it easy to read but still interesting in itself. Of course, you'll only get Internet traffic from members of the communities you drive through, but it all starts there.

Tip Number 75: Forwarded e-mails, modified.

The idea here is to piggyback your URL into the older form of viral media – forwarded e-mails. Supposedly-cursed chain mail aside, these forwarded e-mails are usually sent to friends and acquaintances because there is some value to them.

You can stick your name and URL inside the original footer and send it to your friends and acquaintances, who will then send it to their friends and acquaintances, ad infinitum. The content of the mail itself may be related to your niche, or it may be the usual inane yet interesting stuff that people like passing around. There will always be that chance that someone will see your link, click it, and get to your website, where the rest of the conversion to opt-in process takes place.

Tip Number 76: Business-inclined social networks.

Social networks like Plaxo and LinkedIn have the usual bells and whistles of personal social networks, but the underlying concept is slightly different. Whereas simple social networks involve making friends and keeping them updated with your doings, these business-inclined social networks are meant to help you build and keep a list of business contacts.

What's great about these business social networks is that people are more inclined to talk about work, money, and the like rather than their babies, weekend getaways, or the latest concert. It's social networking filtered by the concept and behavior of the members, optimizing it for business usage. Needless to say, the people you meet here will automatically be useful in your list of contacts.

Tip Number 77: BitTorrent distribution.

Whereas lots of marketers send their wares via direct download links, you can make good use of peer-to-peer distribution systems like BitTorrent. The best strengths of BitTorrent are that it is free, and that downloaded copies will always be available, as long as the downloaders stay connected to the network. No worrying about what will happen if your file host service goes down!